TIME FOR KIDS READERS

SCHOOLS
LONG AGO AND TODAY

by Lisa Trumbauer

Harcourt

Orlando   Austin   Chicago   New York   Toronto   London   San Diego

Visit *The Learning Site!*
www.harcourtschool.com

This is a school **long ago**.

This is a school **today**.

Long ago, children sat in **rows**.

Today, children sit in **groups**.

Long ago, children wrote on **slates**.

Today, children write on **paper**.

Today, children also write on **computers**.